May 25, 1958

To Gail Dumont,

Our congratulations on winning the coveted regional scholarship and our best wishes for your success at Radcliffe.

Franklin and Deborah Haines

D1431617

Rainer Maria Rilke

The Duino Elegies

translated
and
illustrated
by Harry
Behn

MT. VERNON
NEW YORK **Peter Pauper Press**

COPYRIGHT
1957
BY
HARRY BEHN

A NOTE ON ELUSIVENESS

WHEN a young primitive approaches maturity he goes into a wilderness to meditate on happiness, suffering, and the improbable finality of death. The elusive meaning of heroism concerns him; the tyranny of hungers; the importance of things, of spirit guardians; the difference between animals and humans; the power of symbols and song.

It may seem strange to think of Rilke, a cultivated European gentleman, as a primitive, and yet these same preoccupations absorbed him beyond any degree that might be called civilized — especially after 1912 when he lived alone in a desolate castle called Duino, in Austria. There, as awakenings might come to a young Sioux in his vigil, occurred the genesis of these ten magical poems.

After World War I, when the Elegies were at last completed, the poet was no longer young. Still, they speak with the timeless voice of a youth who has seen Angels.

How may another mind absorb so elusive, romantic, intense, and personal a vision? Possibly only as one submits to music. It is essential to have this one key: to Rilke, the things of this world become real by being named. So completely a poet he was. To him, the ultimate immortals are words.

In the Ninth Elegy, he dares at last to name Death, his own death; in the Tenth, to live it, with all the sadness of leaving the earth he loved. By naming and accepting sorrow, he attains immortality and release.

These poems are not at all what we call modern poetry, with its dense intellectual content to be dug free. Digging is no way to experience the Duino Elegies, elusive as they are, as life is, or music. Think about them later. For now, yield to them as lyric intuitions.

The
Duino
Elegies

THE FIRST ELEGY

Who, if I cried out, would heed me amid
    the host
of the Angels? Still, should an Angel exalt
and fold me into his heart I should vanish,
lost in his greater being. For beauty is only
a seed of dread to be endured
yet adored since it disdains to destroy us.
An Angel, alone, is misted in dread,
constraining the shadowy longing
of my lament. Alas, whom do we trust
to sustain us? Not Angels. Not men.
Nor the animals growing aware
that we in a world of illusion
are homeless. Alone
on a cliff stands a tree to be daily
observed; and ours are the charted
streets of the past and the intimate clinging
    of habit
so much at ease with us it will never leave.
Oh, and the night, O night of wind
sated on distance, nibbling our faces; whom
does she not desire, disenchantress,
    being desired,

to leave the desolate heart but a bitter ease.
What consolation is this to a lover?
Out of your arms toss desolation
into the open space we breathe
that birds may perceive an expanded air
beneath their wings as they fly.

Springs greatly desired you. Many a star
waited your gazing upon it to glimmer. A wave
poised toward you yearning in the primal sea;
or as you passed an open window a violin
yielded its soul. For all was a bond.
But were you deserving? Or were you forever
shattered by omens portending the coming
of one desired? (How could you hide
or evade her tenuous image moving
out and in.) Desire as you may,
sing always of love; in the fame
of the greatest love there is little enough
      immortal.
Sing the forsaken, sing whom you faintly envy,
greater are they than those requited.
Unfold their legend now anew, of love
      unattained;
as on the hero marches, his desolation

a pretext only to stride toward his ultimate
       birth.

Lovers embraced by exhausted nature
are wholly absorbed, as though she had lost
her power to revive them. Do you remember
Gaspera Stampa. Would ever a virgin
eluded by love, in such a moment of passion
cry out aloud: I would I were she?
Should not these sorrows of ours
bear fruit at last? Is it not time to be free
of the one desired, in trembling endured:
as the arrow endures the string, in its outward
flight becoming more than it is.
Remaining is nowhere.

Voices, voices. Hear, O my heart, as only
the holy hear: a cry, a shout
lifting them clean of the earth, as they kneel,
impossibly, in rapt meditation:
so must you listen. Not daring to know
the murmur of God, not even afar. But the
       breathing
hear, the legend heed as it wells in silence
rustling toward you from the youngest dead.
In a church in Naples or Rome

were you not whispered to by their fate,
or graven with immortality
as though you were stone, a tomb
      in Santa Maria Formosa.
What do they ask of you? Let them erase at last
a tinge of injustice that hinders
their purely proceeding spirits.

Strange to inhabit the earth no longer,
no longer to use ways newly acquired,
no more to interpret a rose as a mortal future;
no more to be upheld in anxious hands:
to lay one's name aside like a broken toy.
Strange to desire no more to desire.
      O strange to see
all that once was woven together drifting
idly about in space.
Yes, death is hard, and dark with delay
before one faces a trace of eternity.
But the living err in their stark definitions.
Angels (they say) at times are unknowing
whether they move among the quick or the
      dead.
Still timeless the torrent tumbles on,
      through one

domain or the other, resounding above them
     both forever.

They need us no longer, those early departed,
weaned from the earth as a child outgrows
the breasts of a mother. But we who demand
sad mysteries in the guise
of release, could we exist without them?
Is it a fable only, that once in mourning for
     Linos
an early wayward music stabbed through the
     numbness
until into space a godlike youth
departed swiftly, into the void resounding
a humming that now enchants and comforts
     and aids us.

THE SECOND ELEGY

An angel alone is misted in dread. Yet, alas,
I still invoke you, deadly birds of the soul,
who know you well. Oh, where are those days
    of Tobias
when one, most luminous, paused
on a simple threshold, dressed for a journey,
no longer appalling (a youth to the youth
who peered from within).
Let that archangel now, that perilous one
    from beyond the stars,
step down: then upward
beating, outbeat our own hearts. Who are you?

Early and favored shapes of Creation,
mountains dawn-tinted, horizons,
pollen of blossoming godhead,
hinges of radiance, arcades, a stair, a throne,
spaces of being, shields of felicity, tumults
of rapture and suddenly, singly,
mirrors: their own outstreaming splendor
into themselves again withdrawn.

So we dispel as we are moved; we breathe
on our breath away; from ember to ember

yielding a fainter scent. Someone may say:
within this room, you in my blood, the Spring
fills me with you. What do we care, he cannot
    hold us,
we vanish within and about him. Those
    beautiful ones,
who shall embrace them? Seeming, forever,
glows in their faces, and fades. Like dew on a
    lawn
at sunrise, all that is ours exhales like heat
from a crucible. O smile, where are you now?
O lifted eyes, warm and alive, O ebbing heart.
But are we so? The savor of space
on which we fade, is it we? Do angels
absorb what is only theirs, their own auras,
or do they waft away
a part of our being? Is there some trace
in their gazing upon us of some dream
in the face of a woman with child? unseen
in their nebulous spinning into themselves.
(Why should they notice?)

Lovers might say, if they dared, miraculous
    words
upon the night. Although the urge

is all to obscure us. Behold, the trees are;
the houses we live in remain. We only
pass like a drift of air.
Everything stands together to hide us. As
    shame,
perhaps, or an inexpressible aspiration.

Lovers, absorbed in each other,
I ask about us. You cling to each other.
Yet, have you proof you do? My hands are aware
each of the other; between them my face
seeks refuge, awarding me slight response.
But who from that would presume to be?
You flourish in rapture, each in the other's
gaze overcome; until you implore:
no more — who under each other's hands
grow like vintage grapes abundant;
waning, emerging: I ask about us.
I know why you touch, touch persists
with never a vanishing of space
you tenderly cover; there you perceive
duration. Until your embraces
evoke eternity. But when you have known
the first encounter, desire
at the window, the tryst in the garden:

are you unchanged? Each to the other's lips
uplifted — touching wine to wine:
O then how strangely the drinker eludes his
     role.

Were you not startled to see on Attic steles
the tact of a mortal gesture? of love and farewell
so lightly pressed on shoulders the figures
     seemed
woven of other fiber than we are? Recall
those torsos firm with power, those weightless
     hands.
We have gone so far, those wise self-masters
     knew:
this only is ours, to touch; more mightily
only the gods may press on us. And that is the
     gods' affair.
If only we might find somewhere a pure,
     contained,
yet mortal strip of orchard of our own
between the stream and stone! For our hearts
     transcend us
as always they do. And we no more
may dream in visions of rest, nor in
some godlike body achieve a greater austerity.

THE THIRD ELEGY

ONE thing it is to sing of love. Another of woe,
that hidden guilty river-god of the blood.
He whom she holds remotely, her lover, what
    does he know
of that high Lord of Pleasure who, in aloneness,
before she has soothed him, as if she were
    nothing,
from what undetectable deeps would exalt
his godhead, rousing the night to infinite
    uproar.
O the blood's Neptune, his terrible trident.
O the dark blast of his breath on the twisted
    shell.
Hear how the night grows fluted and hollow.
    You stars,
from you springs the lover's delight to behold
his desire. Does not his intimate peering
into her purest face derive from the purest star?

Never did you, O woe, nor his mother
bend his brows to this span.
Never on yours, O maiden, never
on yours did his lips assume that fruitful curve.

Roam like the wind, do you still believe
your delicate nearness it was so shattered him?
You startled his heart; but older fears
awoke in that tremulous touch. Call to him.
        Call.
You cannot entice him far from his somber
        companions.
He tries to escape them; he cannot, and settles
within your heart, weightless,
there to create himself.
But was he there engendered?
Mother, you made him in small, began him;
new in your gaze, as over his eyes you spun
a kindly world, averting a world that was
        strange.
O where is that time when simply you set aside,
with your slender being, the moiling abyss?
Shielded, the nightly frightening room
made harmless; out of your own serene harbor
rippling a known dimension into the night.
Not only in darkness but in your nearness
you placed the friendly beam. Nowhere
a creaking but you would define it
as though you had known when the floor
        would speak . . .

He heard and was calmed
as you came to him; tall and stately, his fate
shrinking behind the bureau; into the rustling
folds of the curtain his furtive future fading
     away.

Tranquil he lay there as under
his lids the warmth of your presence
fashioned a promise of sleep —
and all was serene . . . But within: who could
     stem
or divert the flood of his source?
No waking awoke in the sleeper; sleeping,
dreaming, in fever: O strange embarkation.
He, the new spirit, timid, was tangled
in roots of the inner event,
in primitive images coiled, a proliferation
of bestial preying forms. He yielded.
And loved. Loved his interior jungle,
that primal voiceless world on whose decay,
green-lit, his heart stood. Loved. And departed
into his own deep roots, and out, in violent
     germination,
his own small birth so soon outlived. Descended
into an older ravine to veins

gorged with his forebears where frightfulness
 brooded.
And he was known by fear, who winked, and
 understood.
Yes, horror smiled . . . Ah, seldom, Mother,
did you so sweetly smile. Why should he not
nurture what smiled upon him. This he had
 loved
before you. As you bore him, it was,
dissolved in the waters buoying the germ,

Not as the flowers do, in one
round of the seasons, we love and lift
immortal sap in our limbs. O Maiden, hear:
we love within us not one, a promise,
but all the zealous brew; not one alone
but all the fathers reposing in us
like range after range of decaying mountains;
all the dry stony river beds of the mothers —
all the vistas under a peaceful or under
a stormy sign — from this, O Maiden, you too
emerged. What is your secret will — to summon
primordial time in your lover. Old awareness
swarming out of forgotten creatures.
  What woman

hating and hurting you. What sinister tribes
disturbed in the veins of the young?
Dead infants crying . . . O gently, gently
yield him trust, and love — O lead him
close to the garden, bestow upon him the night
for balance . . .

       Constrain him . . .

THE FOURTH ELEGY

O TREES of life, when does your winter come?
We are not simple. Not as birds are,
strict in migration. Tardy, spent,
we lift on a wind
and are beaten down to the mire.
Diverted, we perish as we flower.
And somewhere lions roam, in their
        magnificence
knowing no weakness.

As we observe the one, we still are aware
of our conquest of the other. Hostility
is near. Are not all lovers
forever wounding the margins of each other
in their pursuit of freedom, of pursuit, of home?
So in a moment's intuition
a base of paradox appears in pain,
that we may see; and all is clear
to us. We know no bounds
of emotion, only the one immediate plane.
Who has not sat before his own heart's curtain?
It lifts: and the scenery is falling apart.
The usual garden,

swaying a little: a dancer.
One dancer. Enough. As he trips about
we probe and discover a merchant
strutting into the kitchen of his home.
I will have none of these harlequin masks,
preferring a puppet. A doll is complete.
Strip off husk and structure of wire and even
the face outside. Hear, hear. I wait
If lights go out, if I am told
there is no more — if from the stage
emptiness pours out like a drift of fog,
or if of all my silent ancestors not one
remains, no woman, not even
a boy with slant brown eyes:
still I stay. One may always stare.

Am I not right? My father, to whom
all life had a bitter taste, my savor,
that first and turbid infusion of my will,
as I grew, with fascination you were always
savoring the aftertaste of so strange
a future, proving my clouded perception —
now you are dead, you stir, my father,
fear in my inmost hope, as peace
owned by the dead, a kingdom of peace

you pay for my crumb of fate,
am I not right? And you, is it true,
whom I should love for that germ
of love for me, from which I turned,
since always the space in your eyes
as I loved it changed into distance
where you no longer were . . . When so I choose
to stand before the stage of the puppets,
to stare so intently my vision at last
is released, as a player appears,
an angel appears and picks up the masks.
Angel and puppet: now there will be a play.
Now what is always dividing
because we are there comes together. At last
out of the cycle of spinning years
the whole design takes form. Above,
an angel soars. Below, the dying,
surely they know how charged with illusion
is all we do here. That all
is not as it seems. O innocent hours,
when more than the past uprose
beyond the players, before us never the future.
We grew, grew easily, impatient
to grow, as much for the sake of those
who had nothing left, except they were grown.

And faring forth in aloneness
we teased ourselves with eternity and stood
on a spot predestined from the start
for a hallowed event.

Who will portray a child as it is? Who place it
among the stars, dole out the measure of
        distance
into its hand? Who will create a child's death
of grey bread that becomes a stone — or leave
a stone in the mouth like the core
of a sweet apple? . . . Murder
is understood. But this, true death,
the whole of death before life
gently holds it, never to be debased,
is beyond description.

THE   FIFTH   ELEGY

Who are they, the acrobats, these hardly more
ephemeral than ourselves, who urgently from
      infancy
are twisted — for the sake
of an ever contending will? Forever it wrings
and bends them, slings and swings them,
tosses and catches them; as out of a well-oiled
smoother air they descend
to the worn carpet, worn by
leaping upon it, tattered, threadbare, lost
in the infinite.
Applied like a plaster, as though suburban
heaven had wounded earth.

                              And scarcely there,
upright and visible: the where,
the vast illumined initial . . . even the strongest
of men are rolled again, in play, by the ever
persistent grip, as August the Strong at table
a tin tray.

O and around
this core the rose of the audience:
blooms and falls. About this

pestle, the pistil, by its own dusty
pollen ensnared,
to the false fruiting
of boredom fertilized,
their never awareness — glinting under a
     delicate
membrane of smirking boredom.

There, the withered, wrinkled strong man,
old and only drumming now,
shriveled within his mighty pelt, as though
it once contained two men, and one
already lain in the grave, and he
had outlived the other,
deaf and a little
weird in his widowed skin.

And the youth, the man, the son of a gnome
and a nun: smartly filled out firm
with muscle and simplicity.

You, with a thud
that fruit know falling unripe
daily a hundred times from the tree of mutually
built up motion, (tree swifter than water,
knowing in minutes Spring, Summer and Fall)

fall and bounce on the grave:
resting, a tenderness
falters over your face out to your seldom
tender mother; over your body spreading
where surface absorbs the trembling
barely attempted expression . . . Again,
a clap of hands for a downward leap,
and before a fear has moved in range of
your galloping heart, the soles of your feet
tingle with leaping, before the impulse to leap
drives out of the eyes a mortal tear.
And blindly, in spite of all,
the smile. . . .

Angel! take it, pluck it, that healing bud of the
      herb vervain.
Mold a jar to preserve it! Set it amid
the not yet open to us delights; in a graceful urn
exalt it with a soaring floral inscription:

                    "Subrisio Saltat."
You then, darling,
you, of all exquisite raptures
mutely blended. Perhaps
your flounces are lucky for you —
or you might feel the virid metallic

hopelessly tattered silk
over taut
young breasts, and want nothing.

You
many a time on the scales in quivering balance
have weighed the fresh fruit of serenity
openly beneath your shoulders.
Where, oh where in the world — perhaps in
          the heart —
are they still far from skillful,
mounting each other, pouncing apart
          like not yet
properly mated animals —
where lifting bars are still heavy
and hoops still wobble
away from vainly
twirling sticks . . . .

And suddenly in this tiresome nowhere,
one precise point where the innocent too little
unaccountably changes — veers
to the vacuous too much.
Where the astronomical account
adds up to zero.

Parks, O park in Paris, infinite theater,
where the modiste Madame Lamort
winds and binds the teeming lanes of earth,
those endless ribbons, to new creations
of frills and flowers, ruffles and artful fruit — all
falsely tinted — for the sleaziest
winter hats of fate.

   .   .   .   .

Angel: imagine a stage of which we know
      nothing, and there
on some indescribable carpet, lovers displayed
      what here
they never may, their daring
lofty designs of aerial sentiment,
pyramids of delight,
ladders where no earth ever was, each only by
      the other
upheld — imagine
before an audience of the innumerable dead:
would they not then toss down their final
      hoarded,
ever concealed, to us unknown, fine minted
golden coins of joy before the ultimate
warmly smiling pair on the hushed
carpet?

THE SIXTH ELEGY

Fᴵɢ tree, long has it held a meaning to me
in the nearly omitted flower;
hiding its purest secret
immured within the timely fruit.
Bough like a fountain driving sap
upward and out: leaping from slumber,
yet scarcely awaking, into the joy of sweetest
    achievement.
Lo, like the god in a swan.
                    .... But as we linger,
alas, we glory in flowering; into the core
of ultimate fruiting we plunge, betrayed.
Few so mightily feel the urge to do
that they stand firm and ripe and radiant
when in seductive dusk the lure to bloom
touches their innocent lips, the lids of their
    eyes:
heroes perhaps and those freed from an
    imminent change whose veins
the gardener Death has altered and coiled.
These surge ahead: triumphant smiles
preceding them, as a team of chargers on the
    mellow

modeled walls of Karnak the conquering king.

Strangely akin to the hero is the youngest dead.
    Continuance
concerns him not at all. His rising is his
    radiance; again
and again he goes forth marching through that
    variable
constellation, his doom. There, few may find
    him. Still,
who darkly deals with us, enraptured fate,
sings him away into the sounding storm of the
    world.
No one like him there is to be heard.
    Through me
his thunders, borne by a tempest, roar.

Then willing am I to escape the longing: Oh
were I a boy to approach and be held
in immaterial arms, to read of Samson
whose mother at first bore nothing and later all.

Was he the hero waiting in you, O Mother,
    beginning there
in you his princely discrimination?

Thousands brewed in the womb
        and wished to be,
but see: he seized and discarded, chose and won.
And when he shattered the portals and burst
from the world of your body into a narrower
        world,
he fared on, choosing and doing. O mothers of
        heroes,
sources of ravaging streams! from high
on the rim of the heart, in despair, down ravines
maidens have plunged, victims of sacrifice for
        the son.
When the hero storms through the hesitations
        of love,
each pulse he awakens, each heart beat
eludes him, apart from smiles he stands,
        a stranger.

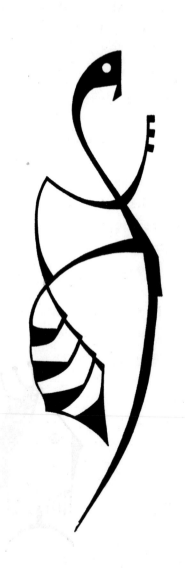

THE SEVENTH ELEGY

Wooing no longer, not wooing, no more
    shall the outworn music
design your lament; though you sigh with the
    note of a bird
when the surging season exalts him, forgetting
    that he
is one more timorous creature and not a
    desolate heart
tossed on the blaze of the blue. As does he,
so should you, no less — arouse
in a mate unseen a slowly awakening
answering voice warmed only by hearing —
your own emboldened emotions glowing in all
    emotion.
O and the Spring would know — no coign
would fail to arouse the tone of annunciation.
    First,
small questioning flutes, and a stillness
investing a purely affirmative day.
Then upward the steps of a call to the dreamt-of
towers of becoming — a trill, a fountain
caught as it rises, caught by its own bright fall
in articulate play . . . And before us, Summer.

Not only a morning of Summer — not only
daybreak emerging into day, before sunrise.
Not only a day gentle among flowers, or above
the formal trees strong and majestic.
Not only the fervor of unfolded powers,
not only avenues, or meadows of evening,
not only, after late thunder, a clearness,
or evening and imminent slumber and
     something surmised . . .
night too! tall summer
nights, and stars, the stars of earth.
O to be dead and know them forever,
all the stars: for how, how, how can we ever
     forget them!

You hear, I have called my love. Not only she
replies . . . Out of compliant graves
a host of maidens appears . . . For how
could I define the note I had sung? The buried
     are always
groping toward earth. — One omen known
may soon be a multitude.
As destiny is only the words of childhood.
How many times in your love were you
     overtaken

breathless on a blissful street into freedom
     without end.
You maidens know, to be here is glorious,
     even you
as you wandered in seeming want, and sank
     in the vilest
alleys of cities, festering.
For an hour was granted to each, not quite
an hour, the measure of time could scarcely
measure between those times she embraced
eternity. All. Veins replete with eternity.
Still, we forget what our laughing neighbor
neither confirms nor denies. What we desire
is seeing. Still, the most visible pleasure
is only revealed when inwardly transformed.
Nowhere, belovéd, can the world be but within.
Life passes in transformation. Ever diminishing,
outwardness disappears. Where once a durable
     house arose,
before us stands a shoddy structure; amid the
     concepts
persistent as though it still were in the mind.
The spirit of time hoards powers, formless,
deep as the urge he draws from out all things.
Temples he knows no longer, the squandering

of meanings we secretly cherish. As on we move,
each treasure tended or knelt to
sighs away unchanging into the invisible
      beyond.
Some never again perceive it and scorn the gain
of building it now anew in grander scale!

Each torpid torque of the world produces the
      disinherited,
owning neither what has been nor what is to be.
The immanent still remote from them. And
      this
must never confuse but empower us in
      holding
close the familiar form. This moved among
      mankind,
stood amid circumstance, the quencher,
      midmost
in aimlessness, as though it was, and bowed
stars toward itself from the established heavens.
      Angel,
I will instruct you! in your perception
it shall appear at last redeemed, upright.
Pillars, pylons, and that Sphinx
      whose groping, grey

above a mouldering temple or a town of
        strangers, aspires.
Is this then not miraculous? O Angel, we are,
we, Mightiness, O tell them, we create! my
        breath
gasps at the wonder. We have never
discarded space the abundant, these
our spaces. (How wonderfully vast they are,
when a thousand years of aspiration cannot
        fill them.)
And yet a tower was tall. O Angel, it was,
tall even compared to you. Chartres was tall —
        and music
arose still higher above and beyond us. Even
a girl in love alone at her window at evening....
does she not reach at least to your knee—?
                        I am not pleading,
Angel, and if I were! You would never appear.
        For calling
is ever full of away; against so strong
a tide one cannot move. Like an outstretched
arm is my call. And its upward reaching
open hand is always before you,
open for warding and warning,
inapprehensible, aloft.

THE EIGHTH ELEGY

With all its eyes the creature world beholds
openness. And still our eyes are turned
in a full circle
like traps ringing the way to freedom.
What lies beyond we only know from the
          animal's
face; for even a child
when turned about and forced to look
at shapes behind it does not see the openness
brooding deeply in the brute face. Free of
          death.
We, only, look on death; the animal's
death is always behind it,
before it, God, and when it moves, it moves
into eternity, as springs run.
Never have we, not for a day,
beheld before us that pure space the flowers
endlessly open upon. Always the world
and never nowhere without no:
the pure untended element we breathe
and always know and never crave. A child
lost in its quietness needs to be startled.
Or someone dies and is openness.

For close to death one no more sees
death, but stares ahead with greater animal
      eyes.
Lovers, were not one or the other always there
clouding the view, are close to death and
      wonder . . .
We glance out carelessly at the revelation,
each behind the other . . . beyond each
no one goes further, and again the world
      returns.
Confronting all Creation, we behold
reflected visions of the free,
but misted by our breathing. Or some animal
lifts its head and calmly stares us through.
So much is destiny: the opposite
and nothing more, always the opposite.

Were there a consciousness like ours
in the precise animal that moves toward us
along another course — would it drag us about
in its wandering. But being itself as it is
it is infinite, not to be known, without a glance
at its own mind, pure, like its gaze,
and where we see only the future, it sees all
and itself in everything and forever healed.

And yet, within the alert warm-blooded beast
there hangs the weight and care of a great
      sadness.
For always to him there clings
what overwhelms us, too — the memory
of what we yearn for still, as it was,
closer, truer, and attached to us
with infinite tenderness. Here all is distance,
there all was breath. After the animal's Eden
the world seems draughty and ambiguous.
O bliss of tiny creatures that remain
forever in the womb that bore them;
O joy of a gnat that still may leap within,
though on its nuptial flight: the womb is all.
Observe the mild assurance of a bird,
though knowing nothing of its source,
the soul of an Etruscan
fled from a corpse in a tomb
carved with a tranquil figure on the stone.
And yet how startled when impelled to fly
is anything that came from a womb. As though
      it feared
itself, zigzagging through the air like a crack
through a cup. So runs the track
of a bat through the porcelain of evening.

And we: spectators always, everywhere,
peering at everything and never out from
    within!
All sates us. We arranged it so. And all decays.
We rearrange it and decay ourselves.

Who has turned us about like this, that we,
do what we may, forever assume the attitude
of one about to depart? As he
on the highest hill who sees his valley
one last time will turn and linger —
so do we live forever taking our leave.

THE NINTH ELEGY

Why do we treasure so highly our moment
        of being that flutters
away like leaves of the laurel, darker
than all surrounding green, with little waves
on every leaf (laughter of wind) — O why
must we, so mortal, avoiding destiny,
sigh after destiny? . . .

                        Not because happiness is true,
that unearned profit of certain loss.
Not from curiosity, or to temper the heart
that still could live in the laurel. . . .
But simply because to live is important, and we
are needed by all this here and now,
these ephemera that oddly concern us.
We most ephemeral. Once
for everything, once only. Once, no more.
        And we, too,
once. And never again. But this
having been, once only:
here on the earth, can it ever again be no more?

And so we continue, trying to be,
to shelter being in our simple hands,

in the crowded eye, the speechless heart.
Try to become. To offer being to whom?
Preferring to hold our being forever . . . Alas,
what can one ferry across? No vision, learned
so slowly, nothing that here has occurred.
Then grief. Above all, the difficult,
the endurance of love —
the unexplainable. And then,
under the stars, what then: that is never
     explained.

Still, the traveler come from a mountain never
     brings
to the valley a clod of unexplainable earth,
     but some
proud word he has won, a yellow and blue
gentian. Are we here merely because we say:
brook, bridge, door, window, tree —
or tower . . . No, but for saying, remember,
O for such saying as never those things
     themselves
hoped so intensely to be. Is not the aim
of this sly earth, in exciting lovers,
to stir all things to leap with their ecstasy?
Say, threshold: what does it mean

to lovers that they should wear their own
worn threshold a little more, they too, after
    the many
before, before those still to come, to be sure.

Now is the time for the word, here is its home.
Speak and make known, now more than ever
things we live with are falling away,
their places taken by deeds without image.
Deeds in a crust that shatters
as powers within outgrow them and other
    events take form.
Between the hammers our heart
lives on, as the tongue
between the teeth, though still
the giver of peace remains.

To the Angel
praise the world but never the inexpressible,
    you
can never impress him with your splendid
    emotions;
he of the infinite knows you are new to them.
    Show
some simple thing that has weathered

until as a part of ourselves it lives in our hands
        and eyes.
Speak to him things. He'll stand amazed: as
        once you stood
beside a weaver in Rome or a potter beside the
        Nile.
Show him how happy a thing can be, how
        guileless and ours,
how even the moaning of sorrow, determined
        by form,
serves as a thing, dies into a thing — as bliss
escapes like a ghost from a violin. These things
        that live
on departure perceive when you exalt them;
elusive, they seek their rescue through us,
most elusive of all.
they want us to change them within our
        invisible hearts
O endlessly — into ourselves! whoever we are.

Is this your wish, O Earth: invisible
emergence in us? Is this your subtle dream,
to become invisible? Earth!
What is your urgent command? to be
        transformed?

Earth, my adored, I obey. You need
no other Springs to win me, one
is more than my blood can endure.
I in your keep have been nameless for aeons.
You have been always right, and your holiest
    vision
friendly death.
Yet I live. On what? Neither my childhood
    nor my future
diminish. . . . . Immeasurable being
wells in my heart.

THE TENTH ELEGY

Emerging one day at last from this
     frightening vision,
may I burst forth in jubilant praise to affirming
     Angels.
May the clear sounding hammers of my heart
fail never by striking slack or
broken strings. May a new glory appear
on my streaming face; an imperceptible
     weeping
burgeon. How good will it seem to me then,
     O nights
of affliction. O inconsolable sisters, why did
     I never
more humbly kneel to receive you, more loosely
yield to your loosened hair. We, wasters of woe.
How we stare at the sad continuance beyond
only to prophecy the end of our sorrows. Yet
     they
are only our winter verdure, our evergreen,
the somber season of our manifest year — not
     only
our season — but pasture, rooted soil, and
     ultimate home.

How strange are the streets of the city of pain.
In seeming stillness out of a mighty din
outdone, out of a mold of emptiness the outcast
struts in gilded fury, a sudden memorial.
How without trace an Angel trod the market
      place
where a church arose all paid for, ready to use,
clean and closed and soulless as a postoffice on
      Sunday.
Still, outside, there billows the fringe of a
      carnival.
Swings of liberty! Divers, jugglers of vigor!
Life-like forms of bedizened glee
to shoot at, targets of tin to tumble and twist
when the marksman scores. From pleasure to
      chance
he reels; to stalls of delight for curious tastes,
touted by bawling and drumming. For adults
      only,
everything visible, well worth seeing,
the breeding of money, not unattractive,
the organs of money — instructive and
      guaranteed
to increase fertility . . . . .
                    Outside,

behind a billboard plastered with placards for
     "Deathless,"
a bitter brew that seems to its sippers sweet,
     so long
as they munch with it tasty distractions . . .
behind the billboard, barely behind it, reality.
Children at play, lovers embracing, and, off at
     one side
in starveling grass, gravely, dogs obeying nature.
Farther the youth is drawn by his love for a
     virgin
lament . . . Into the shadow he follows. She says:
It is far. We live out here . . .

                 Where? And the youth
follows, drawn by her manner. Shoulder,
     throat —
she may be a princess. And yet he leaves her,
     returns,
turns round, and nods . . . What's the use. She's
     only a sorrow.

Only the youthful dead in their first
and timeless indifference
follow her lovingly. Girls
she waits for. Gently shows them

what she is wearing. Pearls of pain and the finest
laces of patience. Beside the young men
she walks in silence.

And where they live in the valley, an older
         lament confides,
charmed by the youth: Time was, she says,
we sorrows were an important family.
         Our fathers
delved in mines in the mountains: among
         the living
at times you find a nugget of polished pain,
or lava from an old volcano, petrified
         anger.
Mined in those mountains. We used to be rich.

And on she leads him through the land
of lamentation, among the ruined columns
of temples, to a palace where long ago
         the first lament
governed the realm. She shows him tall
tear trees, and fields of blossoming woe,
(known to the living only as tender leaves)
shows him pasturing herds of grief — till a bird
shrills in alarm, flashing over his eyes,

its flight tracing the tenuous scrawl
    of its desolate cry.
At twilight, on to the tombs of the eldest
of all her tribe, the sibyls and prophets of doom.
As night falls, silent they move, and the moon
arises, watching, a guard. A brother to him
beside the Nile, the Sphinx, the secret silent
    grave's gaze.
And they are startled by that kingly head,
forever silent, weighing the countenance
of man on the scale of the stars.

His sight unsteady still in death
declines to see. But in her gaze awakens
beyond the double crown an owl. And the bird
strokes him deftly along the cheek,
along its ripening curve
tracing the new perceptive
hearing of the dead, as though on the open
double page of a book, the indefinable outline.

Aloft, the stars. New stars in the land of pain.
Slowly she names them: Lo,
The Rider, Staff, and a milder constellation,
Garland. Onward, toward the pole: The Cradle,
Book of Flame, The Way, The Window.

And in the southern sky, pure as the palm
of a holy hand, the clear resplendent M,
sign of the Mothers. . . .

Onward the dead must move, and the silent
eldest lament attends him as far as the gorge
in moonlight, on to the fountain
of joy. She names it in awe: In the land
of the living this is a mighty stream.
And they stand at the base of the mountain.
And there she embraces him, weeping.

Alone, he climbs to the peak of primal pain,
and never once his passing is heard on the
      soundless way.

If they might stir within us, those timeless dead,
a symbol, they would point to the drooping
seeded pods of the hazel — or show us
rain on dark earth falling in early Spring.

And we who had thought of happiness
ascending would know the emotion
that mildly startles us
when happiness descends.

THIS VOLUME IS DESIGNED
PRINTED AND PUBLISHED
AT THE OFFICE OF
THE PETER PAUPER PRESS
MOUNT VERNON
NEW YORK